VOCAL SELECTIONS

Cover Artwork: Doug Johnson, courtesy DRG
Project Manager: Sy Feldman
Book Art Layout: Joann Carrera

THE HISTORY OF *High Society*

For the 1938–39 Broadway season, Philip Barry, the playwright with a clever talent for drawing room comedy, wrote a stage play about a young woman's discovery of the human being beneath the cool, arrogant virtue of a daughter of the upper classes. She relentlessly holds everyone up to the austere standards she has set for herself. Having already made one bad marriage to a man unworthy of her pride, she is now ready to try again with a self-made man of commerce moving up in the world. Of course, a number of things get in the way right up to the ceremony. In the end, the girl with the good mind and the disciplined body finally acquires the understanding heart of a woman, and the marriage quickly turns into a reunion with the first husband.

Behind the scenes of this brilliant stage hit (in a season that included *The Little Foxes, The Man Who Came to Dinner, The Time of Your Life* and *Life With Father*) became the stuff of show biz lore. Katharine Hepburn had had a string of flops in Hollywood and her share of failures on Broadway when she decided to go back to the stage in a play expressly written for her by Barry. From the very start, Ms. Hepburn proved a savvy investor when she retained the motion picture rights. The Broadway show marked a turning point in Ms. Hepburn's long career. From instant stardom in 1932, the height being an Academy Award in 1933, to the depths, being dubbed "box-office poison" by movie exhibitors in 1938.

The Philadelphia Story opened March 28, 1939, and was a smash hit. Ms. Hepburn remained with the show and took it on tour where it made its way to the West Coast. Once the movie studios saw the show, the bids came in for the rights. MGM was, at that time, the obvious studio to do the film. Always one to negotiate her own deals, the story goes that Ms. Hepburn went to visit Louis B. Mayer at the Culver City lot, was ushered into the grand office, sat down, propped her feet on his desk and asked what he had to offer. On top of a deal that would rival many of her colleagues in the motion picture industry, the condition she held most firmly was that she, and she alone, would play Tracy Lord in the film. In his usual way, Mayer surrounded her with two of his top leading men of the day—James Stewart and Cary Grant—and the rest is history.

High Society was the brightest entertainment (and biggest moneymaker for MGM) of 1956, a rare instance of a musicalized remake proving as good as the original. The success of the film was that screenwriter John Patrick and director Charles Walters never let the music stray from the story. The film starred Frank Sinatra, Bing Crosby and the soon-to-be H.R.H. of Monaco, Grace Kelly. For the screenplay, Cole Porter found eight places where he felt new songs could be added. There was a desire to have Sinatra and Crosby sing together, so Walters suggested a song he, himself, sang with Betty Grable in Porter's 1939 Broadway musical *DuBarry Was a Lady.* "Well, Did You Evah?" with new lyrics tailored to the crooners was, indeed, a high point of the film.

In 1997, a stage production of *High Society* was mounted by the American Conservatory Theatre in San Francisco. The book by Arthur Kopit was based on the play and filmusical, additional lyrics were supplied by Susan Birkenhead and it starred Melissa Errico.

Some sixty years later, *The Philadelphia Story,* now known as *High Society,* finally returned to Broadway when the show opened at the St. James Theatre April 27, 1998.

—Dan O'Leary

Photofest

Photofest

CONTENTS

HIGH SOCIETY

Words and Music by
COLE PORTER
Additional Lyrics by
SUSAN BIRKENHEAD

Very brisk ♩ = 192

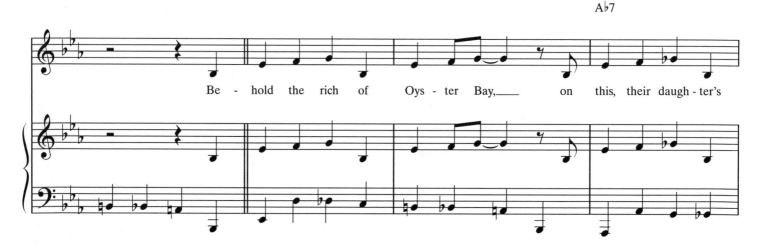

Be - hold the rich of Oys - ter Bay,___ on this, their daugh - ter's

High Society - 6 - 1
0404B

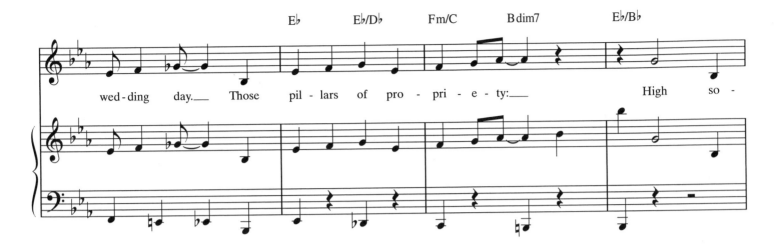

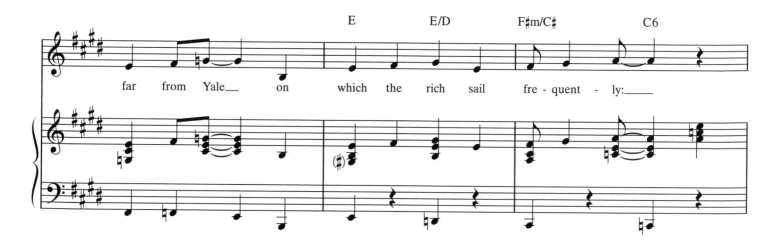

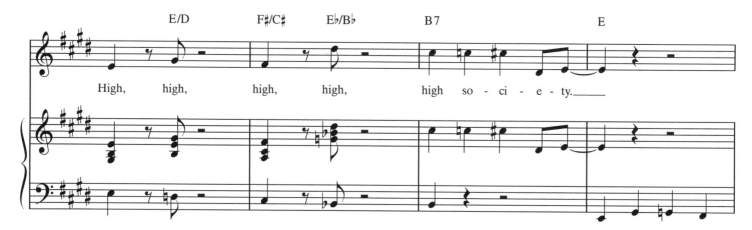

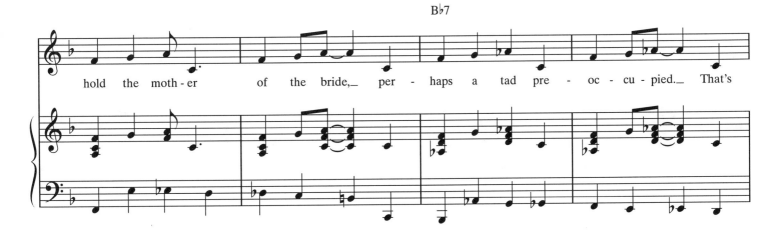

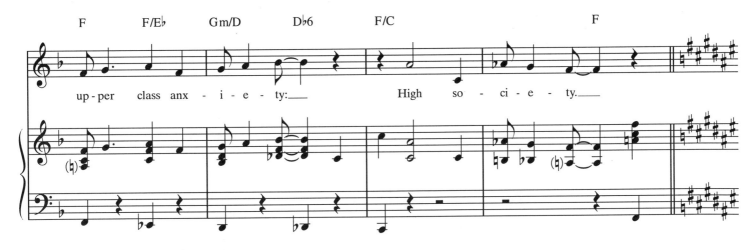

8

hold the sib-ling sulk-ing there,_ her face a mask of dark de-spair._ What

prompt-ed this? Can't wait to see:_ High so - ci - e - ty._

High so - ci - e - ty._ And

Slower ♩ = 144

now the bride to end all brides,_ she swims, she sails, she golfs, she rides. A

Tempo I

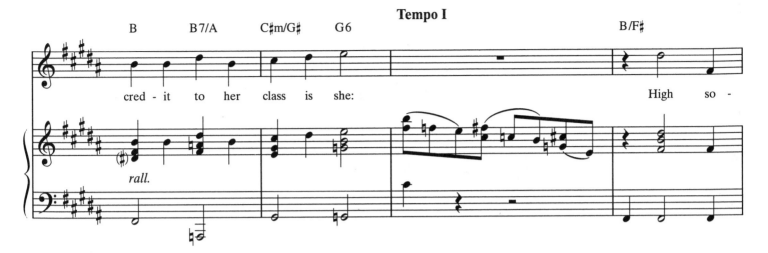

cred - it to her class is she: High so -

ci - e - ty.____

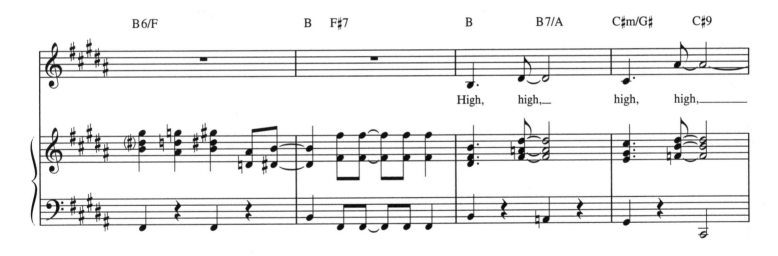

High, high,___ high, high,____

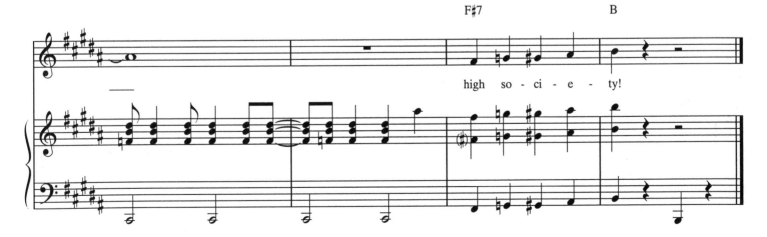

high so - ci - e - ty!

RIDIN' HIGH

Words and Music by
COLE PORTER

Allegro non troppo

LITTLE ONE

Words and Music by
COLE PORTER

Refrain:

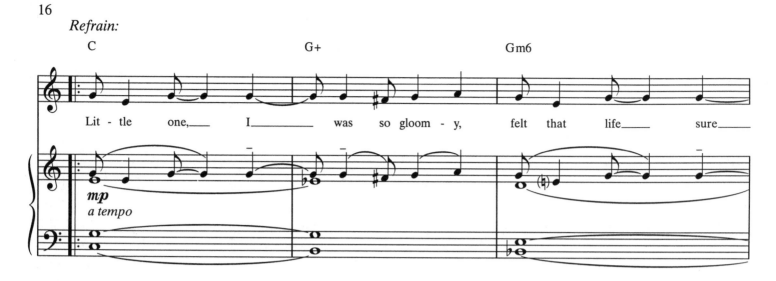

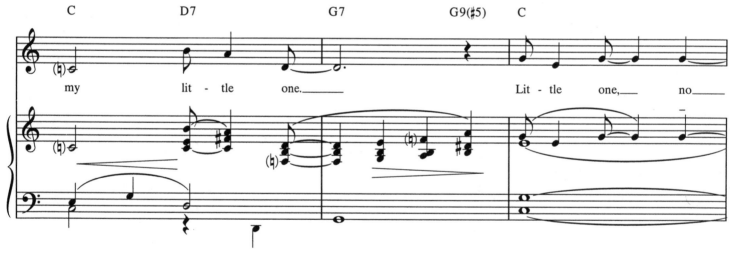

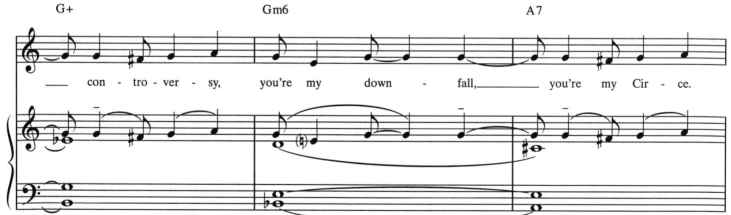

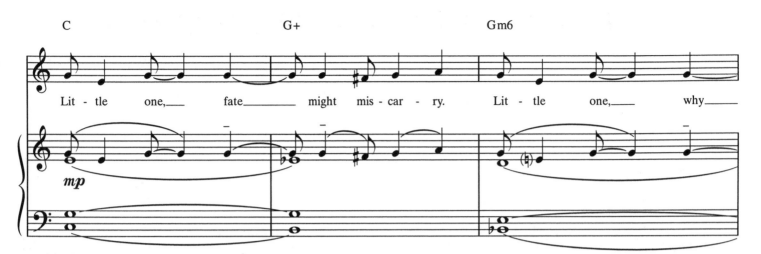

Little one,___ fate___ might mis-car - ry. Lit - tle one,___ why___

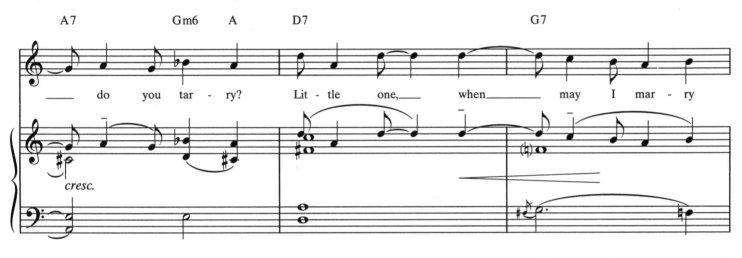

___ do you tar - ry? Lit - tle one,___ when___ may I mar - ry

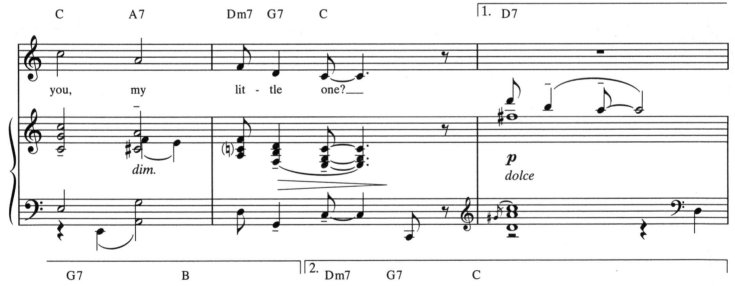

you, my lit - tle one?___

WHO WANTS TO BE A MILLIONAIRE?

Words and Music by
COLE PORTER

Moderato

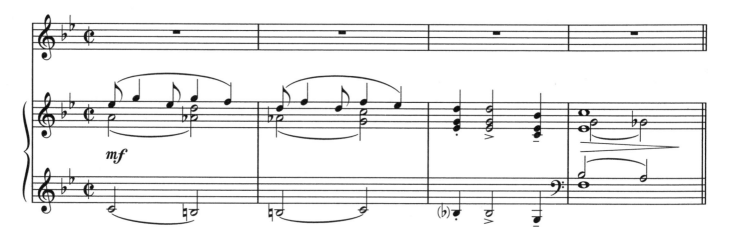

Verse:

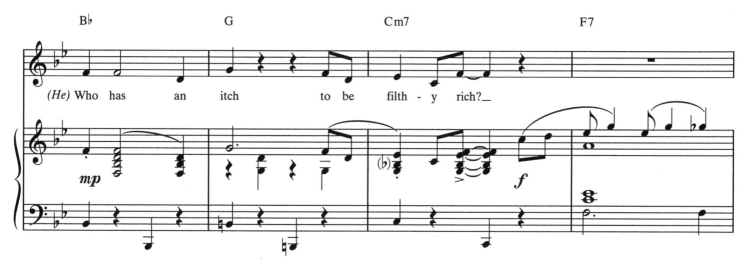

(He) Who has an itch to be filth-y rich?__

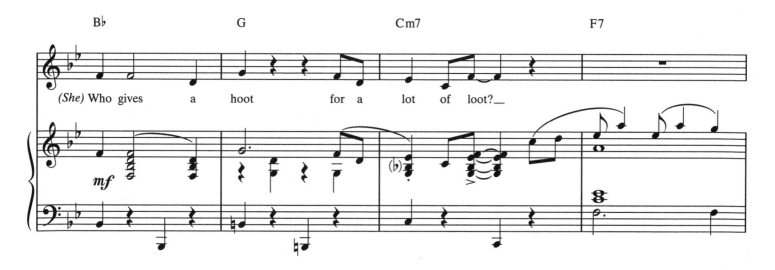

(She) Who gives a hoot for a lot of loot?__

Who Wants to Be a Millionaire? - 4 - 1
0404B

I LOVE PARIS

Words and Music by
COLE PORTER

I love Par - is in the win - ter, when it driz - zles. I love Par - is in the sum - mer, when it siz - zles. I love Par - is ev - 'ry mo - ment,_____ ev - 'ry mo - ment of the year._____

Cm

C

C/E   E♭dim7   G7   Dm7   G7

TRUE LOVE

Words and Music by
COLE PORTER

LET'S MISBEHAVE

Words and Music by
COLE PORTER
Additional Lyrics by
SUSAN BIRKENHEAD

In slow fox-trot time

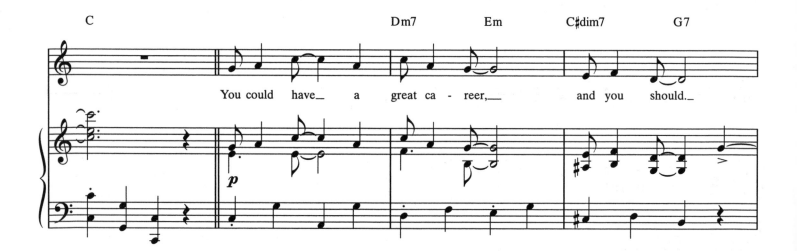

You could have a great ca - reer, and you should.

Let's Misbehave - 5 - 1
0404B

Refrain:

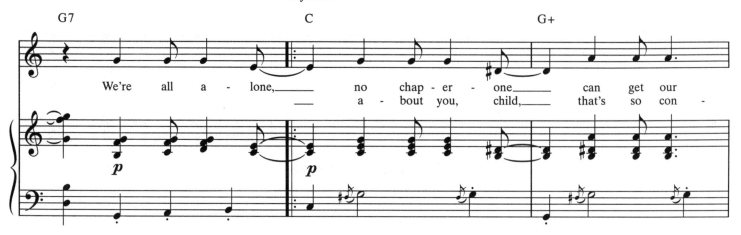

We're all a - lone,____ no chap - er - one____ can get our
____ a - bout you, child,____ that's so con -

num - ber. The world's in slum - ber,
ta - gious. Let's be out - ra - geous,

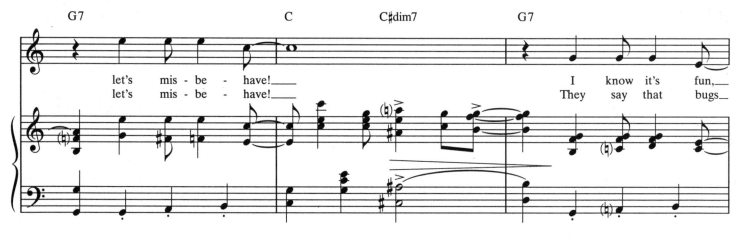

let's mis - be - have!____ I know it's fun,____
let's mis - be - have!____ They say that bugs____

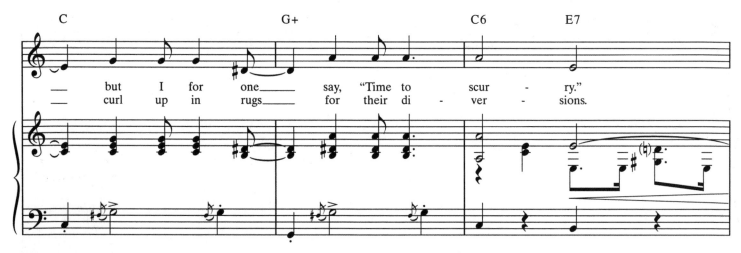

____ but I for one____ say, "Time to scur - ry."
____ curl up in rugs____ for their di - ver - sions.

34

JUST ONE OF THOSE THINGS

Words and Music by
COLE PORTER

Moderately

It was just one of those things,

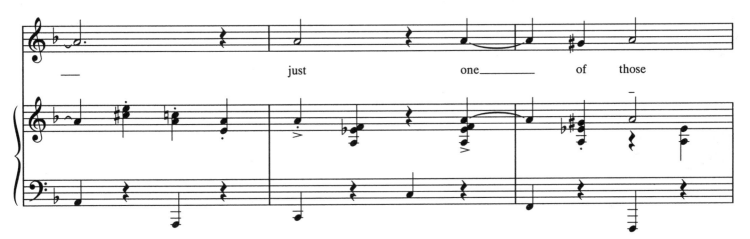

just one of those

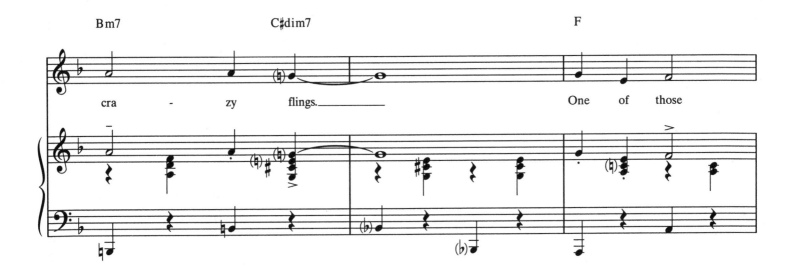

cra-zy flings. One of those

Just One of Those Things - 5 - 1
0404B

bells that now and then rings,

just one_____ of those things._____ It was

just one_____ of those nights,_____

just one_____ of those fab - u - lous

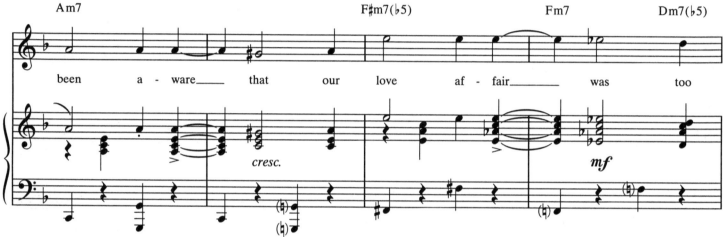

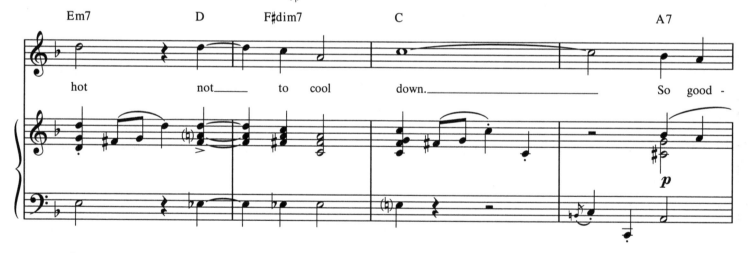

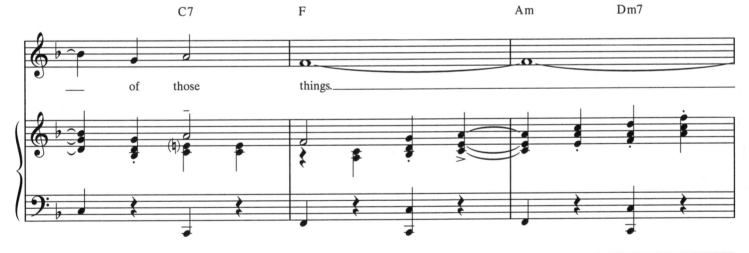

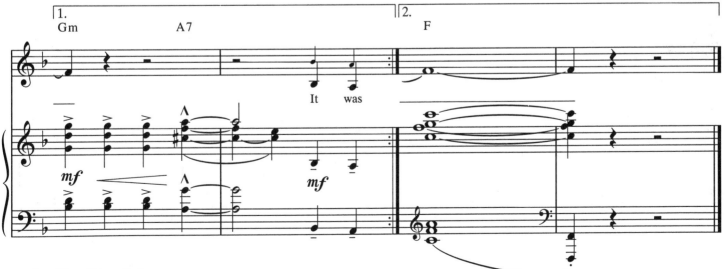

WELL, DID YOU EVAH?

Words and Music by
COLE PORTER
Additional Lyrics by
SUSAN BIRKENHEAD

Tempo di polka

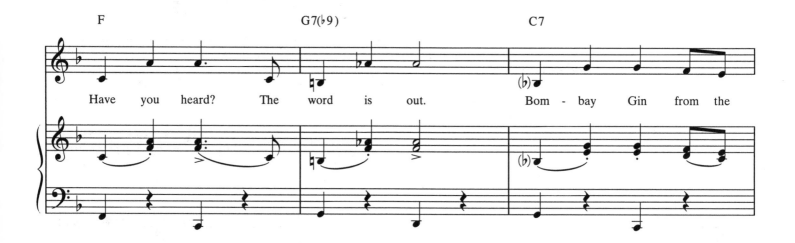

Have you heard? The word is out. Bom-bay Gin from the

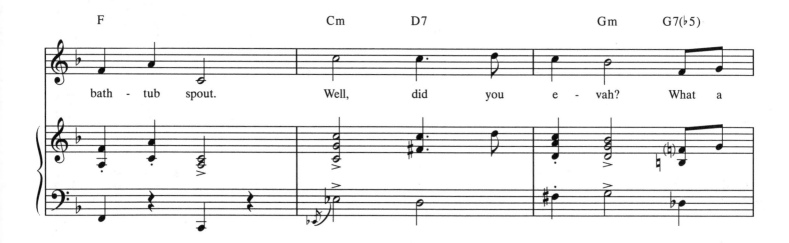

bath-tub spout. Well, did you e-vah? What a

Well, Did You Evah? - 4 - 1
0404B

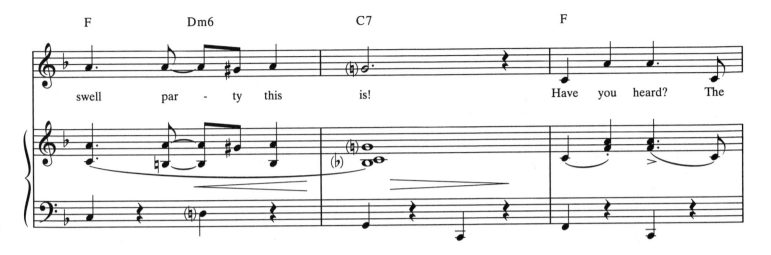

swell par - ty this is! Have you heard? The

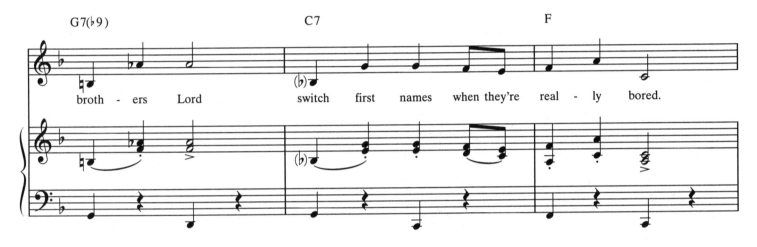

broth - ers Lord switch first names when they're real - ly bored.

Well, did you e - vah? What a swell par - ty this is! How

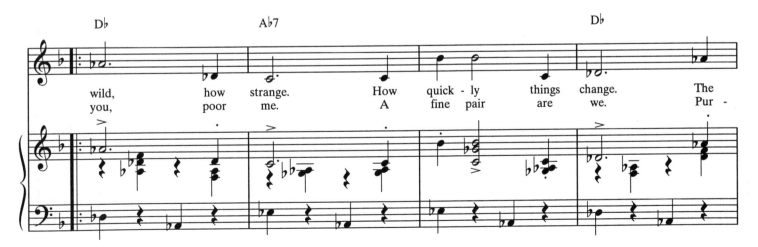

wild, how strange. How quick - ly things change. The
you, poor me. A fine pair are we. Pur -

moon? Who knows. Cham - pagne? I sup - pose. How
sued like prey. The catch of the day. What

wrong. How right. How mid - sum - mer night. A
fun! It's not. That's right, I for - got. Ah,

free - for - all. The al - che - my of al - co - hol.
well I know. *But* *thank you, God, for* *veuve clic - quot!*

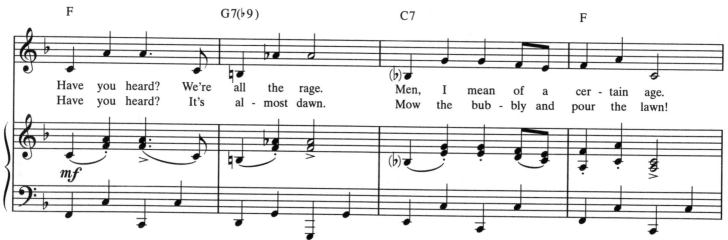

Have you heard? We're all the rage. Men, I mean of a cer - tain age.
Have you heard? It's al - most dawn. Mow the bub - bly and pour the lawn!

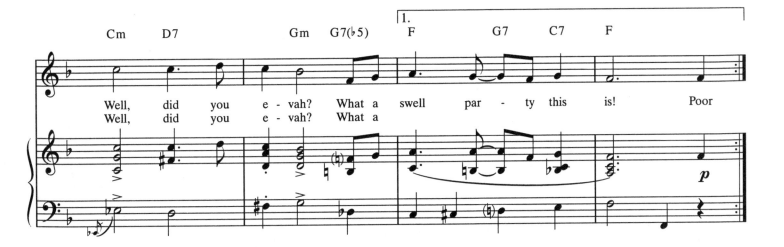

Well, did you e-vah? What a swell par-ty this is! Poor
Well, did you e-vah? What a

swell par-ty this is! Have a drink, in fact, have two!

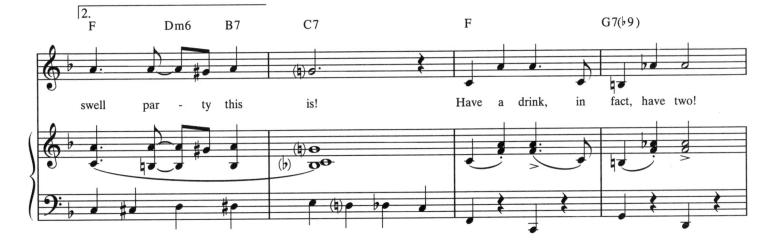

Don't look now, but we've had a few! Well, did you e-vah? What a

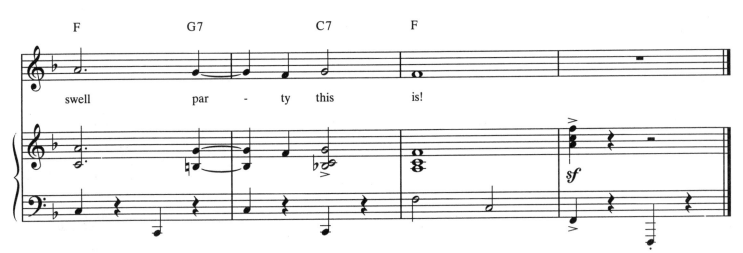

swell par-ty this is!

YOU'RE SENSATIONAL

Words and Music by
COLE PORTER

IT'S ALL RIGHT WITH ME

Words and Music by
COLE PORTER

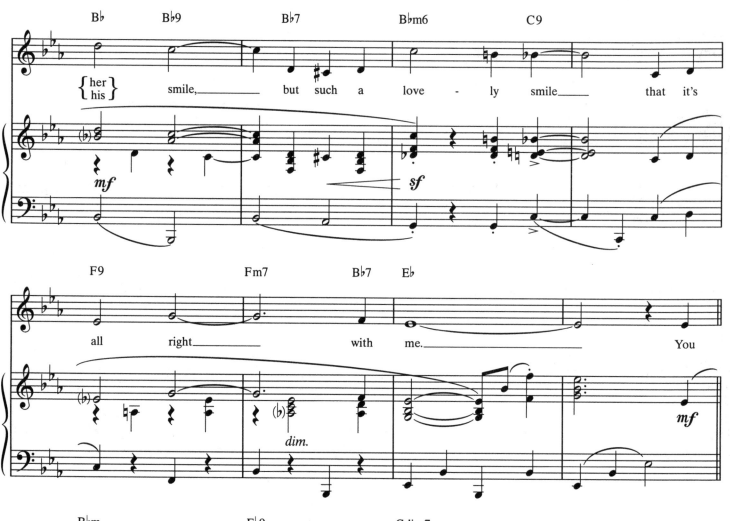

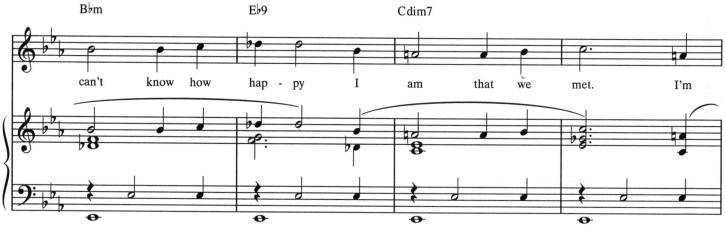

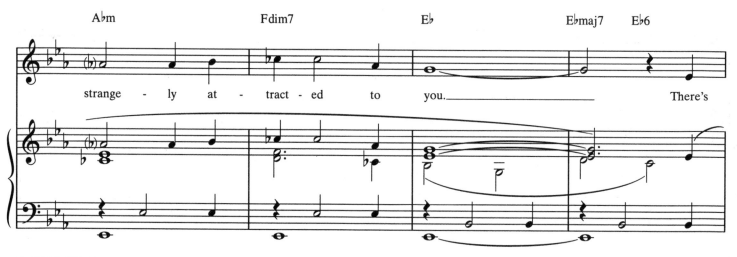

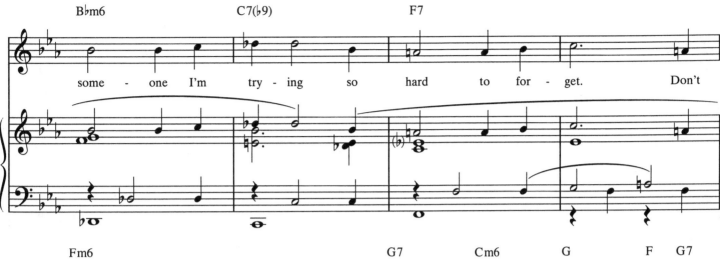

some - one I'm try - ing so hard to for - get. Don't

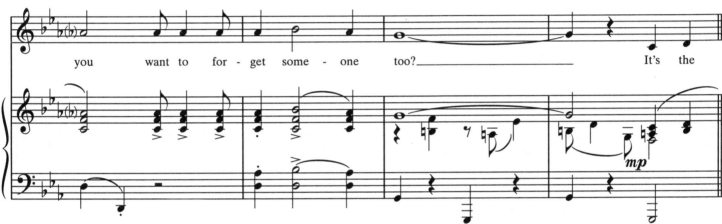

you want to for - get some - one too?_____ It's the

wrong game_____ with the wrong chips. Though your

lips are tempt - ing, they're the wrong lips. They're not

I LOVE YOU, SAMANTHA

Words and Music by
COLE PORTER

Refrain:

love you,_____ Sa - man - tha,_____ and

my love_____ will nev - er die._____ Re -

mem - ber,_____ Sa - man - tha,_____ I'm a one

gal guy._____ To - geth - er,_____

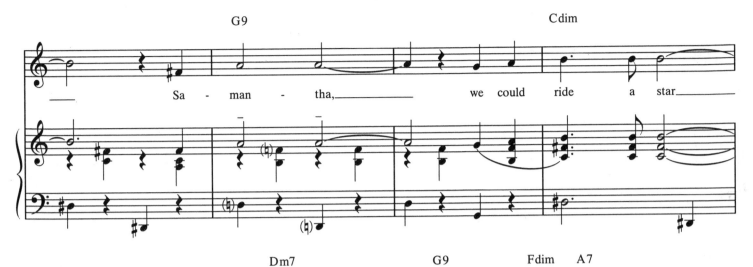

I Love You, Samantha - 4 - 3
0404B

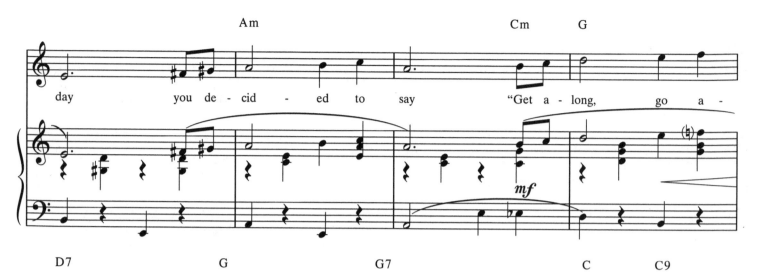

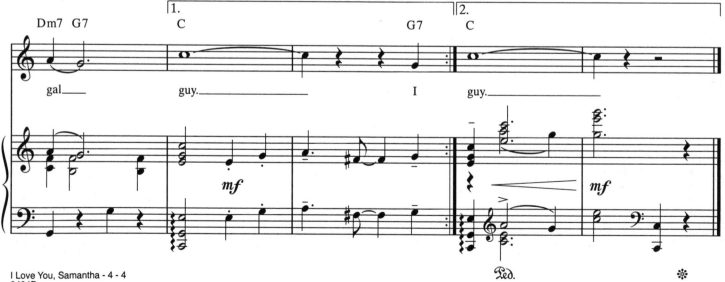